Contents

T0087327

Part I

Part II

PART I:
THREE OCTAVE SCALE FINGERING ALTERNATIVES
FOR THE VIOLIN
by Paul Rolland

Compiled and Edited, with an Introduction,
by Dr. James Starr, Emporia State University

Introduction

The name of Paul Rolland needs little introduction: Distinguished pedagogue and artist of his time, widely published, and important founding member, president, then publications chair, and active supporter to his death of the American String Teachers Association. He also founded the ASTA JOURNAL and served as its editor for many years. His death in 1978 left a huge void in the string teaching world. However, his films, publications, and ideas continue to live on to help and inspire the modern string teacher.

As with any active, creative person, some of his work and materials remained unpublished and hence unavailable to the general public when he died. When I worked actively with Professor Rolland as a doctoral student during the years 1971–1975, he used two series (major and melodic minor) of three octave scale fingerings with me for technical exercises that he had developed. These fingerings were based primarily on half-step shifting, and he felt these were easier to learn than the traditional three octave scale fingerings used by other pedagogues—most of which used whole-step shifting quite freely. In his series of fingerings, or **fingering alternatives,** as he called these, the principle of the half-step shift was adhered to quite consistently in most major scales, while whole-step shifts were used only in secondary, or alternate, fingerings. In the melodic minor scales, half-step shifts were used unless a whole-step shift could not be avoided. The two abiding principles emphasized in his **alternatives** were fluency of shifting over the entire fingerboard and establishing more accurate intonation. To achieve fluency, Rolland emphasized not only half-step shifting, but bowings using different rhythmic groupings or patterns—to force a person to concentrate on the bowings. Then a student could gradually learn to shift cleanly and effortlessly with the left hand by doing so almost automatically, because he/she would be compelled to concentrate on the bowings in rhythmic groups! The three octave scales consequently became also bowing exercises that the teacher and student could use to plan and use parts of or the entire length of the bow to play a specific number of notes at a time. The use of the scales for improving and perfecting the bow arm was a unique way in which Mr. Rolland combined the aspects of left and right arm technique. He had created an excellent plan to emphasize what he believed to be of primary importance—developing and perfecting the bow arm. Using the scales to do so, he exemplified his constant attention to this area of violin technique. He himself had an excellent bow arm and was always a good example to his students.

In the following pages, one will find each of Rolland's fingering alternatives—first with the fingering alone, each then followed by the appropriate scale or scales that can be used with this fingering written in notation, with Rolland's first suggested fingering added. This way the teacher and students may use either or both according to their choice or need. In addition, at the end of all the fingerings and bowings of Part I, I have included a two page summary of all the Rolland fingering alternatives showing just fingerings. A student, having previously studied the various fingerings, may then wish to use these summary pages as short review sheets and for warm-ups.

I wish to gratefully acknowledge the cooperation and support of Paul's beloved wife Clara in allowing me to examine many of Paul's personal unfinished materials in preparation for this project.

James A. Starr: January 29, 1999

Three Octave Scale Fingering Alternatives for the Violin

Part I: Major and Melodic Minor Scales
by Paul Rolland

Compiled and Edited, with an Introduction
by Dr. James Starr, Emporia State University

Part II: Harmonic Minor Scales
by Dr. James Starr

BOOSEY $\mathscr{C}$ HAWKES

AN IMAGEM COMPANY

DISTRIBUTED BY

HAL•LEONARD®
CORPORATION

7777 W. BLUEMOUND RD. P.O. BOX 13819 MILWAUKEE, WI 53213

ISBN 978-0-913932-74-2

THREE OCTAVE MAJOR SCALE FINGERING ALTERNATIVES:

Scale Fingering No. 1: G Major

The following scale should first be practiced with separate bows, one count to a note, in the middle of the bow. The dashes between fingerings indicate half-step shifts, except at the upper end of the scale, where **4-4-4** indicates a repeated fourth finger extended a half step up and then brought back down a half step. The dotted lines (..........) between fingerings indicate that the player should continue fingering in consecutive order without shifting until reaching the next written fingerings. In the written-out version of each scale, the standard designation of the broken line (∧ or ∨ between notes) is used to designate half steps.

Fingering: (no shifting until the E String)
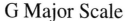
```
      G          E                              G
     012............01-123-1234-4 (stop) 4-4321-43210...............0
```

After playing the scale a few times, or when playing the scale faster, eliminate the stop and the repeated note at the top of the scale.

G Major Scale

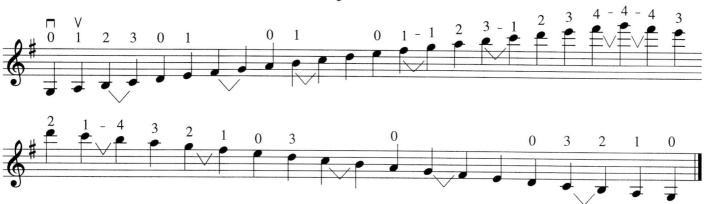

Alternative Fingering No. 1: (no shifting until the E String)
```
      G          E                              G
     0............1234-1234-4 (stop) 4-4321-4.........0
```

Alternative Fingering No. 2:
```
      G   A*   E                         *    G
     0.....12-1....12-1234-4 (stop) 4-4321-214321-2 ...0
```
(Note: * above a dash indicates a whole-step shift)

Bowing Variations to be used with this and succeeding scales:

Bowing 2: Slur three notes in a bow (quarter notes) slowly. Work towards the use of the entire bow, one third of the bow per note.

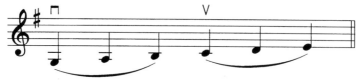

Bowing 3: Slur three notes in a bow faster (eighth-note speed), middle "half" of the bow (one fourth below, one fourth above) or more, as practical.

Bowing 4: Slur six notes in a bow (eighth notes), whole bows.

Bowing 5: Slur six notes in a bow faster (sixteenth notes), middle two thirds of the bow. Think two groups of three in each bow for ease of counting.

Bowing 6: Slur nine notes in a bow (sixteenths), full bows. Think three groups of three for counting purposes.

Bowing 7: Slur twelve notes in a bow (sixteenths), full bows. Think four groups of three for counting.

Bowing 8: Slur half of the scale in a bow, fast sixteenths: three octaves up in one bow, stopping on top note; three octaves down in one bow, stopping on bottom note. Think and feel groups of three as you proceed.

Bowing 9: Play the full three octave scale, up and down, in one bow—fast sixteenths, carefully saving the bow. Use one half bow for the scale going up and one half bow going down. Thinking groups of three may help to plan bow use.

Note: Bowings 8 and 9 should only be attempted after one is thoroughly fluent and familiar with bowings 1-7.

Alternate bowings to Bowings 2-7:

Bowing 2a: Slur four notes to a bow (quarter notes) slowly, whole bows, one fourth of the bow to a note.

Bowing 3a: Slur four notes to a bow (eighth notes) faster, in the middle three fourths of the bow.

Bowing 4a: Slur eight notes to a bow (eighth notes), whole bows. Think groups of four for counting purposes.

Bowing 5a: Slur eight notes to a bow (sixteenth notes), reasonably fast, in the middle three fourths of the bow (two groups of four in each bow).

Bowing 6a: Slur twelve notes in a bow (think three groups of four while counting), reasonably fast sixteenths, whole bows.

Bowing 7a: Slur half a scale in a bow as before in Bowing 8, thinking and feeling groups of four as you proceed.

Bowing 8a: Slur the whole scale in a bow, as in Bowing 9, thinking and feeling groups of four as you go.

More advanced bowing and rhythmic concepts:

After the above bowings and rhythmic concepts are learned, memorized, and played fluently, the student may, at the discretion of the teacher, try more difficult rhythmic groupings for counting and coordination of fingers and bow, such as the following:

Slurring five notes in a bow, slow and fast, thinking 3+2, 2+3, or five.

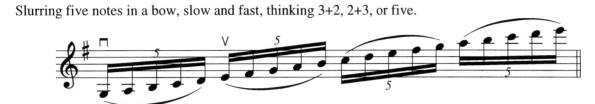

Slurring seven notes in a bow, slow and fast, thinking 4+3, 3+4, or seven.

Slurring ten notes in a bow, counting 3+3+4, 4+4+2, and other combinations.

Slurring thirteen notes in a bow, counting 3+3+3+4 or other combinations.

Slurring sixteen notes in a bow, counting four groups of four.

Slurring two notes to a bow fast, either starting in twos or playing one note in the first bow and twos thereafter.

Playing combinations of so many slurred notes followed by so many separate notes, such as 2+2, 3+3, 4+4, 2+3, 3+2, 4+2, etc.

Scale Fingering No. 2 (scales beginning on the first finger: A and A♭ Major):

Fingering:

<pre>
  G   E   G
  1 .... 12-123-1234-4 (stop) 4-4321-321-2 1
</pre>

A Major Scale

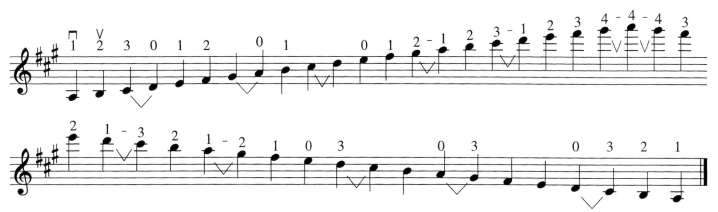

Alternate fingering:

<pre>
  G   A   E   A (A)   G
  1 ...... 12-1 ...... 123-1234-4 (stop) 4-4321-3214 .. 1-2 ... 1
</pre>

(Descending scale fingerings may be exchanged.)

Ab Major Scale

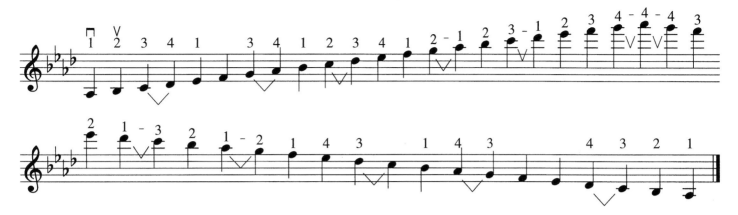

Scale Fingering No. 3 (scales beginning on second finger: Bb, B, Cb, C, C#, and Db Major):

Fingering:

```
        G           E                                    G
        2 .......... 3-123-1234-4 (stop) 4-4321-321-321 ......... 2
```

Bb Major Scale

Alternate fingering:
```
        G        A        E                        A        G
        2 ..........3-1 ..........3-1234-4 (stop) 4-4321-3214321-3 ..... 2
```

(Descending fingerings may be exchanged.)

B Major Scale

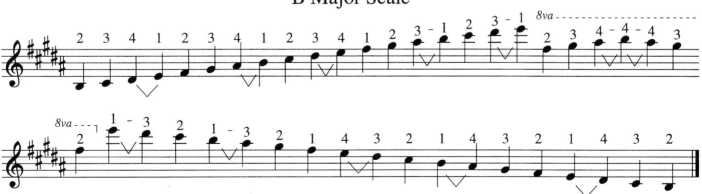

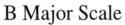

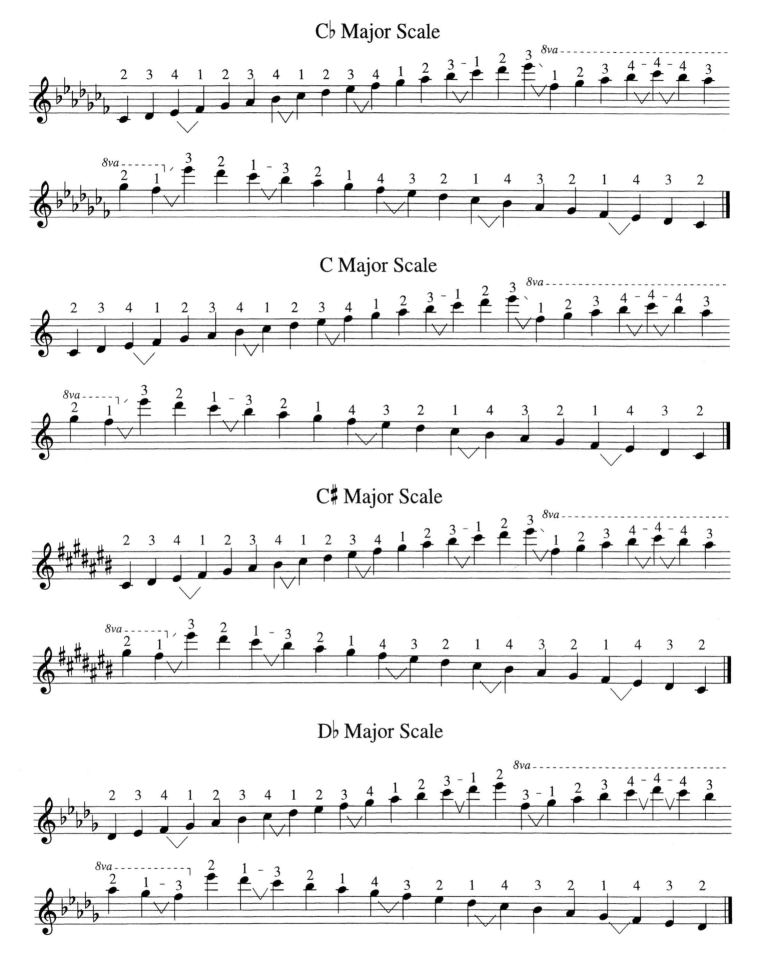

C♭ Major Scale

C Major Scale

C♯ Major Scale

D♭ Major Scale

Scale fingering No. 4: D Major: Begin on open D String.

Fingering:

D   A   E   A   D

0 .... 2-1 .... 3-123-1234-4 (stop) 4-4321-321-3214321-2 0

D Major Scale

Scale fingering No. 5 (E and E♭ Major): Begin with first finger on the D String.

Fingering:

D   A   E   A   D

1 ....3-1 .... 3-123-1234-4 (stop) 4-4321-321-3214321-3 1

E Major Scale

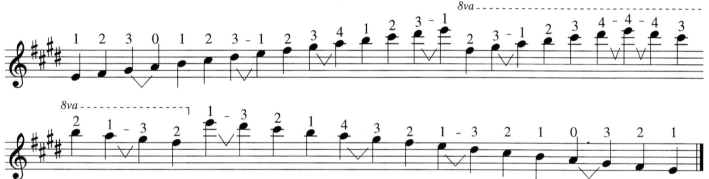

E♭ Major Scale

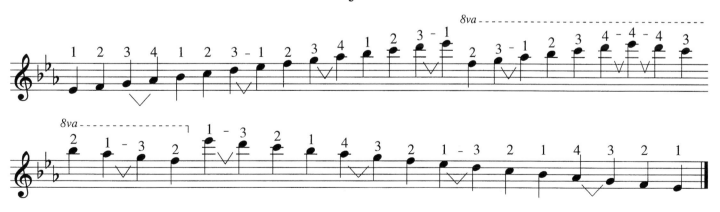

Scale fingering No. 6 (F, F♯, and G♭ Major): Begin with second finger on the D String.

```
D        E                                          A    (A)     D
2 ........ 3-1234-123-1234-4 (stop) 4-4321-321-3214321-4 ..... 2
```

F Major Scale

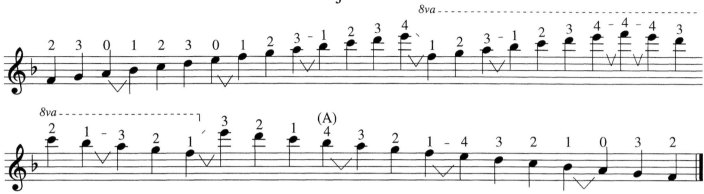

F♯ Major Scale

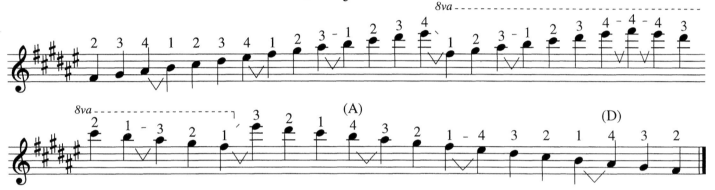

G♭ Major Scale

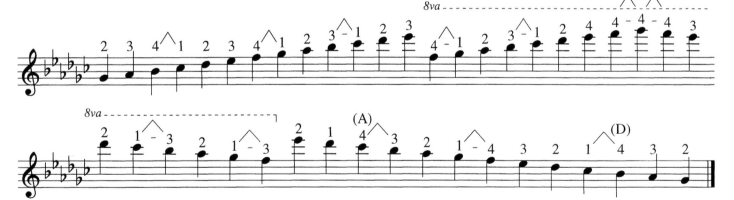

Alternate fingering:

```
D     A     E                                      A   (A)    D
2 ..... 4-1 ..... 3-123-1234-4 (stop) 4-4321-321-3214 .. 1-4 ..... 2
```

THREE OCTAVE MELODIC MINOR SCALE
FINGERING ALTERNATIVES:

Important Note: An asterisk (*) over a shift indicates a whole-step shift.

Scale Fingering No. 7: G Melodic Minor:

Fingering:

```
      G    A *       E *                                    G
      0 ..... 12-1 ..... 12-1 ..... 4-4 (stop) 432-321-3 .......... 0
```

G Melodic Minor Scale

Alternate fingering: **(Note: Excellent fingering, without shifts until the E String — Editor)**

```
      G              E        *                             G
      0 ................ 1-123-1234-4 (stop) 432-321-3 ........... 0
```

Scale Fingering No. 8: Starting with first finger on the G String (A, A♭, G♯, and A♯ Melodic Minor):

Fingering:

```
      G          E        *                             G
      1 ............... 12-123-1234-4 (stop) 432-321-4 ........... 1
```

Alternate fingering:

```
      G      A        E        *                                 G
      1 ........ 1-1 .......... 1-123-1234-4 (stop) 432-321-4 .................. 1
```
Also possible descending:
```
                                              E        A        G
                                              432-3214321-21 ..... 1-21
```

A Melodic Minor Scale

A♭ Melodic Minor Scale

G♯ Melodic Minor Scale

A♯ Melodic Minor Scale

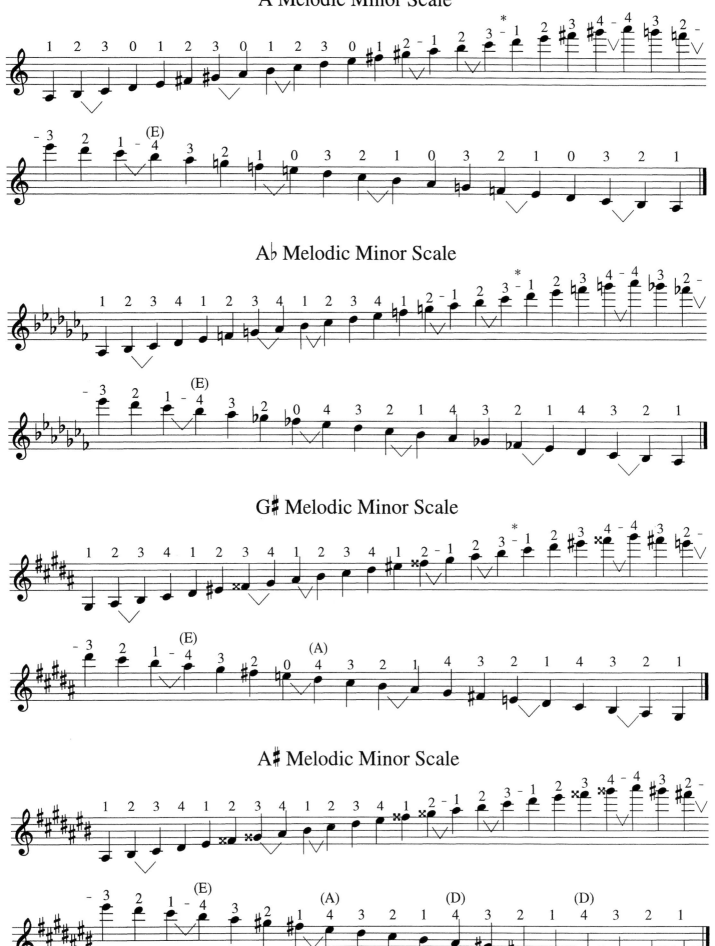

Scale Fingering No. 9: Starting with second finger on the G String (B, B♭, C, and C♯ Melodic Minor):

Fingering:
```
      G           E      *                                A          G
      2 ............ 3-123-1234-4 (stop) 432-321-3214321-2 ..... 2
```

B Melodic Minor Scale

Alternate fingering:
```
      G      A       E      *                          A      D      G
      2 ......2-1...... 1-123-1234-4 (stop) 432-3214321-3214321-2... 2
```

(Descending scale fingerings are interchangeable.)

B♭ Melodic Minor Scale

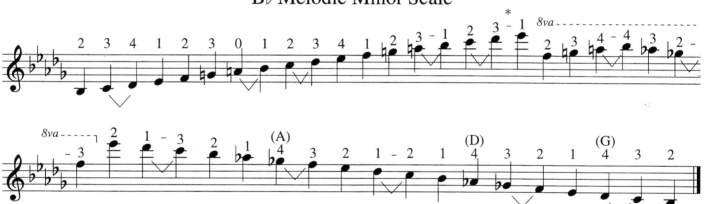

C Melodic Minor Scale

C♯ Melodic Minor Scale

Scale Fingering No. 10: Starting with Open "D" (D Melodic Minor):

Fingering:

```
        D       A       E       *                        A           D
        0 ...... 2-1 ...... 3-123-1 .... 4-4 (stop) 432-321-3214321-4 ........ 0
```

D Melodic Minor Scale

Scale Fingering No. 11: Starting with first finger on the D String (E, E♭, and D♯ Melodic Minor):

Fingering:

```
        D       A       E       *                        A       D       D
        1 ........ 3-1 ........ 3-123-1234-4 (stop) 432-321-3214321-3214321-21
```

E Melodic Minor Scale

E♭ Melodic Minor Scale

D♯ Melodic Minor Scale

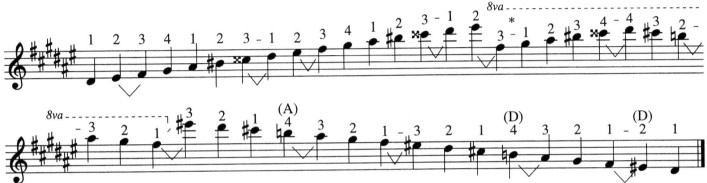

Editor's Note: At this point in the Rolland manuscript of melodic minor fingering alternatives, the fingerings end. It is obvious, however, that one final fingering alternative for three octave melodic minor scales was not included by Mr. Rolland in his manuscript: scales beginning with the second finger on the D String (f and f♯ minors). He may not have had time to finish the series. Whatever the reason, I have written a fingering for these final two scales myself to make the series complete. I have tried to maintain the same general principles of fingering and shifting that Mr. Rolland used in the previous scales.

Scale Fingering No. 12: Starting with second finger on the D String (F♯ Melodic Minor):

Fingering:
```
    D  A  E      *        *                    *    A      D
    230123412-1234-123-12-234-4 (stop) 432-321-321-43214321-21032
                                                  *E      A      D
    or alternative descending fingering:         -4321-210321032
```

F♯ Melodic Minor Scale

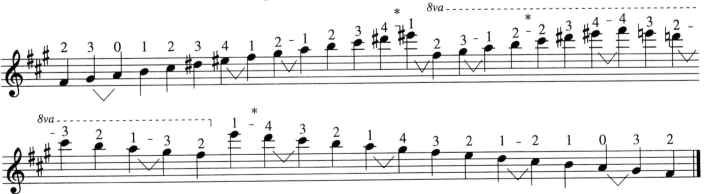

Scale Fingering No. 13 (F Melodic Minor):

Fingering:

```
     D   A   E        *        *                        *    A        D
     234123012-1234-123-12-234-4 (stop) 432-321-321-43214321-21432
                                                      *E       A    D
     or alternative descending fingering:            -4321-214321432
```

F Melodic Minor Scale

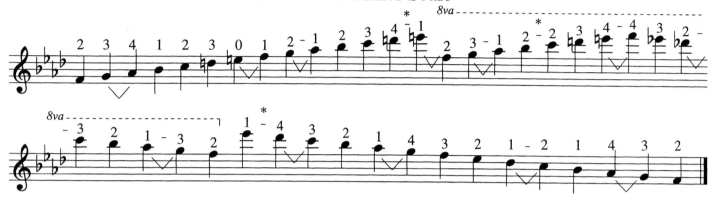

Summary: Three Octave Major Scale Fingering Alternatives

1. G Major.

    a) G   E   G
        0 .... 1-123-1234-4 (stop) 4-4321-4 0

    b) G   E   G
        0 .... 1234-1234-4 (stop) 4-4321-4 0

    c) G   A *   E   A *   G
        0 .... 12-1 .... 12-1234-4 (stop) 4-4321-214321-2 0

    (* indicates whole-step shift — Editor)

2. Begin with first finger (A and A♭ Major).

    a) G   E   G
        1 .... 12-123-1234-4 (stop) 4-4321-321-2 1

    b) G   A   E   A (A) G
        1 ..... 12-1 ..... 123-1234-4 (stop) 4-4321-3214 .. 1-2 ... 1

    (Descending scale fingerings may be exchanged.)

3. Begin with second finger on G String (B♭, B, C♭, C, C♯, and D♭ Major)

    a) G   E   G
        2 .... 3-123-1234-4 (stop) 4-4321-321-321 2

    b) G   A   E   A   G
        2 ..... 3-1 ..... 3-1234-4 (stop) 4-4321-3214321-3 2

    (Descending fingerings may be exchanged.)

4. Begin on open D String (D Major).

        D   A   E   A   D
        0 .... 2-1 .... 3-123-1234-4 (stop) 4-4321-321-3214321-2 0

5. Begin with first finger on D String (E and E♭ Major).

D		A		E		A		D
1	....	3-1	....	3-123-1234-4 (stop)	4-4321-321-3214321-3		.....	1

6. Begin with second finger on D String (F, F♯, and G♭ Major).

a)
D		E		A	(A)	D
2	....	3-1234-123-1234-4 (stop)	4-4321-321-3214321-4		.....	2

b)
D	A		E		A	(A)	D
2	....	4-1	......	3-123-1234-4 (stop)	4-4321-321-3214	.. 1-4	.....	2

Summary: Three Octave Melodic Minor Scale Fingering Alternatives

Note: An asterisk (*) over a shift indicates a whole-step shift.

1. G Melodic Minor scale fingering.

a)
G		A *		E *			G
0	.....	12-1	.....	12-1	..... 4-4 (stop) 432-321-3	....	0

b)
G		E	*		G
0	....	1-123-1234-4 (stop) 432-321-3		....	0

2. Begin with first finger on G String (A, A♭, G♯, and A♯ Melodic Minor).

a)
G		E	*		G
1	....	12-123-1234-4 (stop) 432-321-4		....	1

b)
G	A		E	*		G
1	....	1-1	....	1-123-1234-4 (stop) 432-321-4		....	1

		E	A	G
Also possible descending		432-3214321-21	.....	1-21

3. Begin with second finger on G String (B, B♭, C, and C♯ Melodic Minor).

a)
G		E	*		A	G
2	....	3-123-1234-4 (stop)		432-321-3214321-2		 2

b)
G	A	E	*		A	D	G
2	......	2-1 ...	1-123-1234-4 (stop)		432-3214321-3214321-2		... 2

(Descending scale fingerings a) and b) are interchangeable.)

4. D Melodic Minor, beginning on open D String.

D		A		E	*		A		D
0	......	2-1	......	3-123-1	.... 4-4 (stop) 432-321-3214321-4			....	0

5. Begin with first finger on D String (E, E♭, and D♯ Melodic Minor).

D		A		E	*		A	D	D
1	....	3-1	....	3-123-1234-4 (stop)		432-321-3214321-3214321-21			

6. Begin with second finger on the D String (F♯ Melodic Minor).

D A	E		*	*			*	A	D
230123412-1234-123-12-234-4 (stop)					432-321-321-43214321-21032				

or alternative descending:
	*E	A	D
	-4321-210321032		

7. Also beginning with second finger on the D String (F Melodic Minor).

D A E		*	*			*	A	D
234123012-1234-123-12-234-4 (stop)					432-321-321-43214321-21432			

or alternative descending:
	*E	A	D
	-4321-214321432		

PART II

THREE OCTAVE HARMONIC MINOR SCALE
FINGERING ALTERNATIVES
by Dr. James Starr

Introductory Note:

The very nature of the harmonic minor scale, with its characteristic one and one-half step interval between the seventh and eighth tones, creates problems for ease of finger placement and smooth shifting over a three octave range, especially as the tempo of the notes increases. The following fingerings have been conceived with Paul Rolland's basic two principles again in mind - fluency in shifting and ease of finger placement to obtain the best intonation. The shifting intervals have been kept as small as possible, and shifts have been chosen that are least awkward ascending or descending. Some shifting sequences that work well ascending seem more awkward descending. Hence, fingering changes have been made. But in other cases, the same sequence can be used ascending and descending. Alternative fingering suggestions have been included in only a few scales (indicated by fingerings in parentheses) because other possibilities were considered to be too awkward. As with Rolland's three octave scale alternatives, the harmonic minor scales should be practiced with the various bowings previously introduced in Part I.

THREE OCTAVE HARMONIC MINOR SCALE
FINGERING ALTERNATIVES:

Key to symbols: -   (between fingerings), means a shift, or movement of the same finger a half step higher or lower.

∧ or ∨   (over a shift or between notes), refers to a half step shift or a half-step interval.

*   (over a shift), means a whole-step shift.

(1½)   (over a shift or between notes) = 1 1/2 steps

N S   Means no shift, only the same finger a half step higher or lower

Scale Fingering No. 14: G Harmonic Minor.

Fingering:

```
   G    D    A    E∧    *                    *    A    D    G
01230123012341-123-1234-4 (stop) 4-4321-43214321032103210
                     N            N
                     S            S
```

G Harmonic Minor Scale

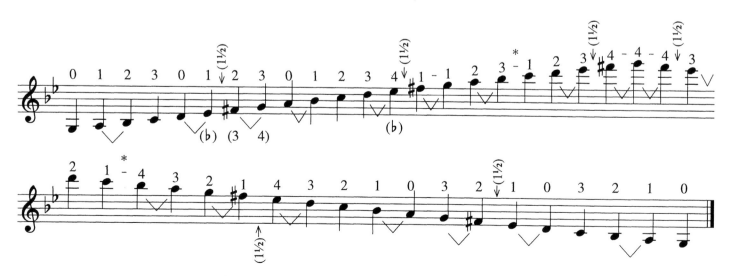

Scale Fingering No. 15: A Harmonic Minor.

Fingering:

```
        G  D  A  E  ^  *                    *        A  D  G
        12301240123012-123-1234-4 (stop) 4-4321-321-21032104210321
                      N         N
                      S         S
```

A Harmonic Minor Scale

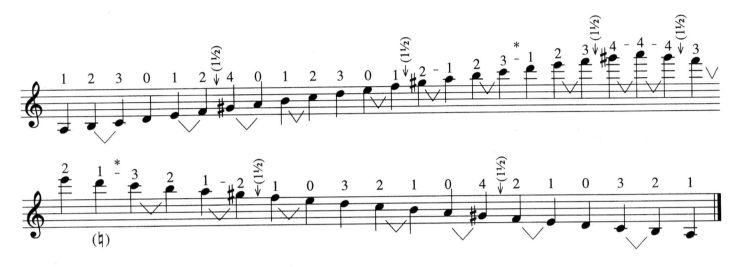

Scale Fingering No. 16: A♭ Harmonic Minor.

Fingering:

```
        G  D  *  A  E  *                   *     A  D  *  G
        123412-12341234123-1234-4 (stop) 4-4321-32143214321-214321
                    N         N
                    S         S
```

A♭ Harmonic Minor Scale

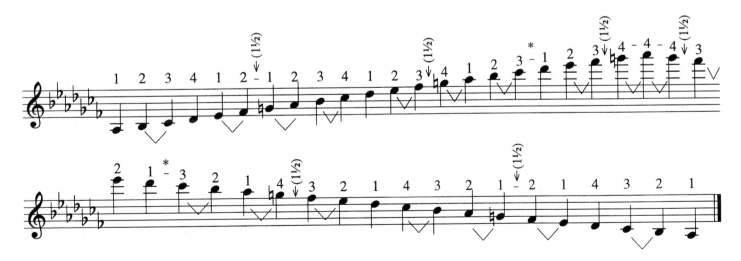

Scale Fingering No. 17: G♯ Harmonic Minor.

Fingering:

G D (1½) A E *   * A * D G
123412-12341234123-1234-4 (stop) 4-4321-3214321-2143214321
              N   N
              S   S

G♯ Harmonic Minor Scale

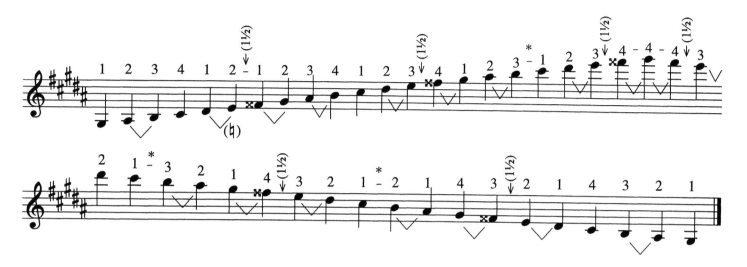

Scale Fingering No. 18: A♯ Harmonic Minor Scale.

Fingering:
G D A * E *   * A * D G
1234120123-1234123-1234-4 (stop) 4-4321-3214321-3210214321
              N   N
              S   S

A♯ Harmonic Minor Scale

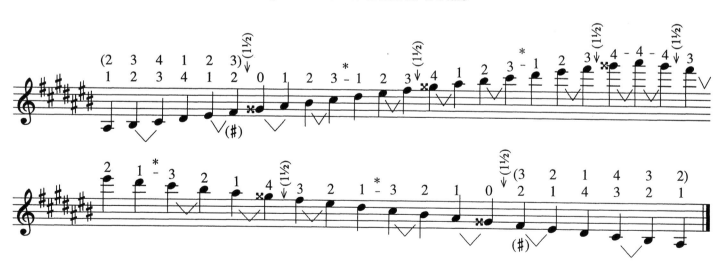

19

Scale Fingering No. 19: B Harmonic Minor.

Fingering:

```
    G D    A    E    ^    *                        *    ^    A    D    G
    2301231-1230123-123-1234-4 (stop) 4-4321-321-4210321-1321032
            N              N         N            N
            S              S         S            S
```

B Harmonic Minor Scale

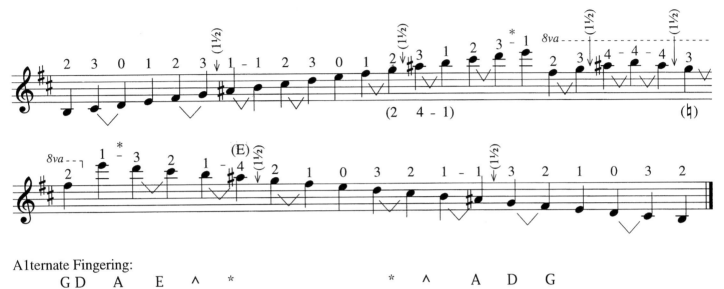

Alternate Fingering:

```
    G D    A    E    ^    *                        *    ^    A    D    G
    2301231-1230124-123-1234-4 (stop) 4-4321-321-4210321-1321032
            N              N         N            N
            S              S         S            S
```

Scale Fingering No. 20: B♭ Harmonic Minor.

Fingering:

```
    G D    A    E    ^    *                        *    ^    A    D    G
    23412301234123-123-1234-4 (stop) 4-4321-321-32143210321432
                N            N
                S            S
```

B♭ Harmonic Minor Scale

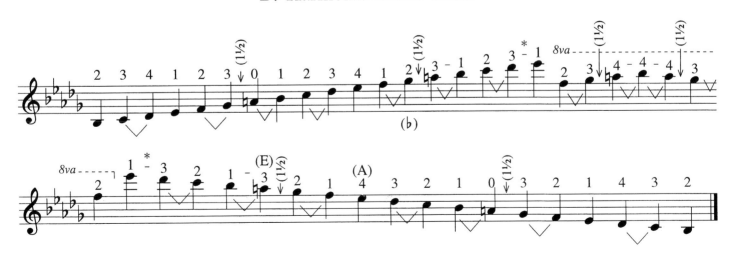

Scale Fingering No. 21: C Harmonic Minor.

Fingering:

```
      G D  A  E  ^  *                    *  ^  A   D   G
      23412341234123-123-1234-4 (stop) 4-4321-321-32143214321432
                     N         N
                     S         S
```

C Harmonic Minor Scale

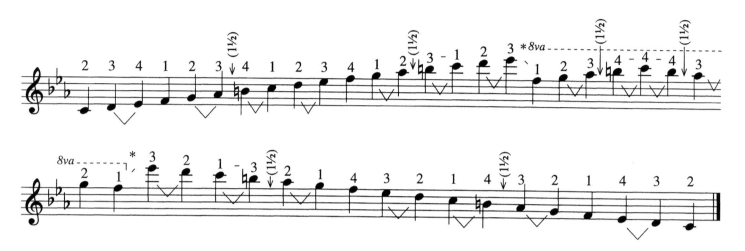

Scale Fingering No. 22: C♯ Harmonic Minor.

Fingering:

```
      G D  A  E  ^  *  *            *  *  ^  A   D   G
      341230123012-123-123-1234 (stop) 4321-321-321-210321032143
```

C♯ Harmonic Minor Scale

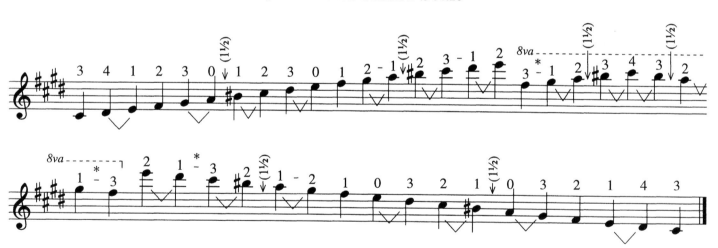

Scale Fingering No. 23: D Harmonic Minor.

Fingering:

```
     D   A   ^   E   ^   *                   *   ^   A   ^   D
     0123012-1234123-123-1234-4 (stop) 4-4321-321-3214321-2103210
                   N           N
                   S           S
```

D Harmonic Minor Scale

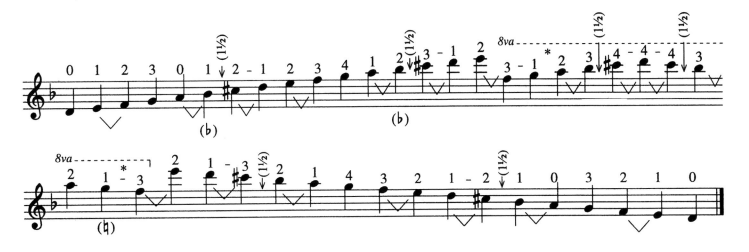

Scale Fingering No. 24: E Harmonic Minor.

Fingering:

```
     D ^   A^   E   ^   *                   *   ^   A   ^   D
     12-12341-1234123-123-1234-4 (stop) 4-4321-321-3214321-4210321
                    N           N
                    S           S
```

E Harmonic Minor Scale

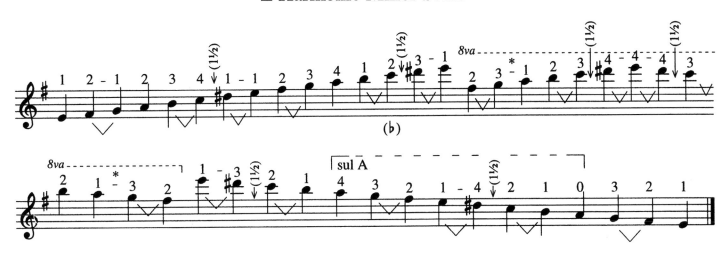

Scale Fingering No. 25: E♭ Harmonic Minor.

Fingering:

```
     D ^      A^    E ^    *                      *    ^    A    ^    D
     12-12341-1234123-123-1234-4 (stop) 4-4321-321-3214321-3214321
                     N            N
                     S            S
```

E♭ Harmonic Minor Scale

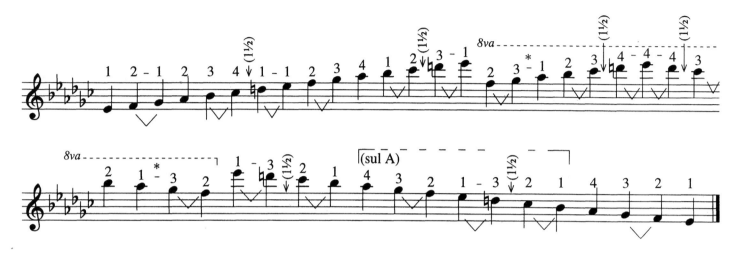

Scale Fingering No. 26: D♯ Harmonic Minor.

Fingering:

```
     D   *    A     E ^    *                    *    ^    A    ^    D
     123-1231-1234123-123-1234-4 (stop) 4-4321-321-3214321-3214321
            N              N      N
            S              S      S
```

D♯ Harmonic Minor Scale

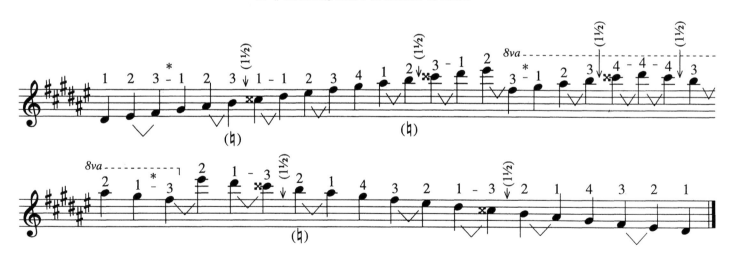

Scale Fingering No. 27: F♯ Harmonic Minor.

Fingering:

```
    D A  ^    E   ^   *  *                    *   ^  ^    A       D
    23012-1234123-123-12-1234-4 (stop) 4-4321-321-31-3214321-21032
                     N          N
                     S          S
                                                 ^E ^   A      D
         Alternative descending fingering:      -321-214321032
```

F♯ Harmonic Minor Scale

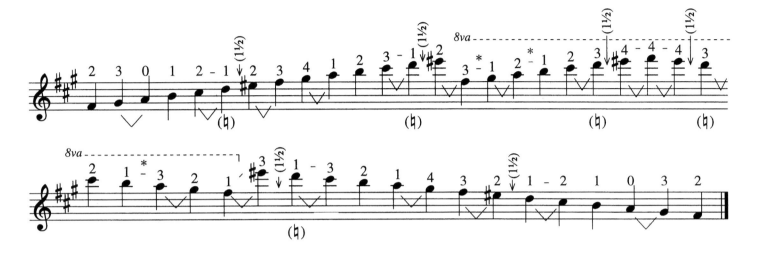

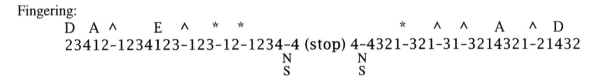

Scale Fingering No. 28: F Harmonic Minor.

Fingering:

```
    D A ^    E  ^   *  *                    *   ^  ^   A  ^  D
    23412-1234123-123-12-1234-4 (stop) 4-4321-321-31-3214321-21432
                    N          N
                    S          S
```

F Harmonic Minor Scale

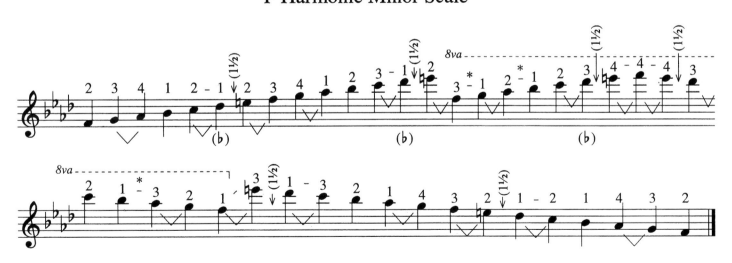

Summary: Three Octave Harmonic Minor Scale Fingering Alternatives

Note: –   means shift or finger extension

$\frac{N}{S}$ means no shift - only a finger extension or pull back of 1/2 step

^   means half-step shift

*   means whole-step shift

$\overset{\frown}{(1\frac{1}{2})}$ means a shift of 1 1/2 steps

1. G Harmonic Minor Scale fingering:
```
     G   D   A   E^  *                        *     A     D   G
     01230123012341-123-1234-4 (stop) 4-4321-43214321032103210
                           N         N
                           S         S
```

2. A Harmonic Minor Scale fingering:
```
     G   D   A   E   ^   *              *   ^   A   D   G
     12301240123012-123-1234-4 (stop) 4-4321-321-21032104210321
                          N         N
                          S         S
```

3. A♭ Harmonic Minor Scale fingering:
```
     G   D * A   E   *              *   A   D   *  G
     123412-12341234123-1234-4 (stop) 4-4321-32143214321-214321
                         N         N
                         S         S
```

4. G♯ Harmonic Minor Scale fingering:
```
            (1½)
     G   D  ⌢  A   E   *              *   A   *  D   G
     123412-12341234123-1234-4 (stop) 4-4321-3214321-2143214321
                         N         N
                         S         S
```

5. A♯ Harmonic Minor Scale fingering:
```
     G   D   A   *   E   *              *   A   *   D G
     1234120123-1234123-1234-4 (stop) 4-4321-3214321-3210214321
                         N         N
                         S         S
```

6. B Harmonic Minor Scale fingering:
```
     G D   A   E   ^   *                   *   ^   A   D   G
     2301231-1230123-123-1234-4 (stop) 4-4321-321-4210321-1321032
          N                 N       N                   N
          S                 S       S                   S
```

Alternate Fingering:
```
     G D   A   E   ^   *                   *   ^   A   D   G
     2301231-1230124-123-1234-4 (stop) 4-4321-321-4210321-1321032
          N                 N       N                   N
          S                 S       S                   S
```

7. Bb Harmonic Minor Scale fingering:

```
     G  D  A    E  ^  *                        *    ^    A      D      G
     23412301234123-123-1234-4 (stop) 4-4321-321-32143210321432
                          N                    N
                          S                    S
```

8. C Harmonic Minor Scale fingering:

```
     G   D   A   E  ^   *                       *    ^    A      D      G
     23412341234123-123-1234-4 (stop) 4-4321-321-32143214321432
                          N                    N
                          S                    S
```

9. C# Harmonic Minor Scale fingering:

```
     G D   A    E  ^    *    *                   *    *    ^    A      D      G
     341230123012-123-123-1234 (stop) 4321-321-321-210321032143
```

10. D Harmonic Minor Scale fingering:

```
     D   A  ^     E  ^    *                      *    ^    A    ^    D
     0123012-1234123-123-1234-4 (stop) 4-4321-321-3214321-2103210
                           N                    N
                           S                    S
```

11. E Harmonic Minor Scale fingering:

```
     D ^     A^    E   ^    *                     *    ^    A    ^    D
     12-12341-1234123-123-1234-4 (stop) 4-4321-321-3214321-4210321
                           N                    N
                           S                    S
```

12. Eb Harmonic Minor Scale fingering:

```
     D ^     A^    E   ^    *                     *    ^    A    ^    D
     12-12341-1234123-123-1234-4 (stop) 4-4321-321-3214321-3214321
                           N                    N
                           S                    S
```

13. D# Harmonic Minor Scale fingering:

```
     D   *    A    E  ^    *                      *    ^    A    ^    D
     123-1231-1234123-123-1234-4 (stop) 4-4321-321-3214321-3214321
           N                  N                    N
           S                  S                    S
```

14. F# Harmonic Minor Scale fingering:

```
     D A  ^     E  ^    *    *                    *    ^  ^    A    ^    D
     23012-1234123-123-12-1234-4 (stop) 4-4321-321-31-3214321-21032
                           N                    N
                           S                    S
```

```
                                                ^E   ^    A      D
     Alternative descending fingering:          -321-214321032
```

15. F Harmonic Minor Scale fingering:

```
     D A  ^     E  ^    *    *                    *    ^  ^    A    ^    D
     23412-1234123-123-12-1234-4 (stop) 4-4321-321-31-3214321-21432
                           N                    N
                           S                    S
```

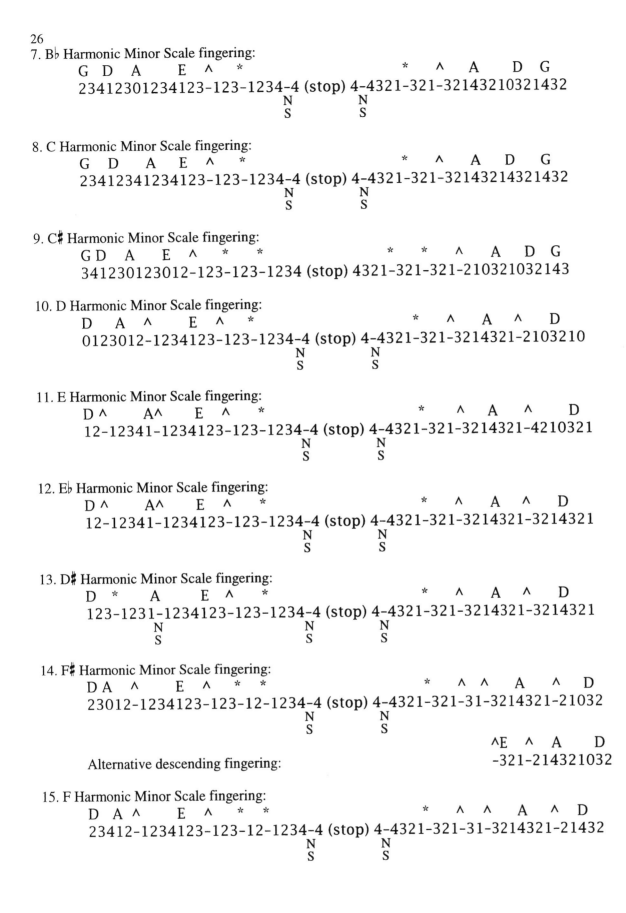